CINZIA RANDAZZO

THE EDUCATION OF THE YOUNG PEOPLE TO THE ORIGINS OF THE CHRISTIANITY

Youcanprint *Self-Publishing*

Title | The education of young people to the origins of the Christianity
Author | Cinzia Randazzo
ISBN | 978-88-91186-62-1

Youcanprint Self-Publishing
Street Roma, 73 - 73039 Tricase (LE) - Italy

www.youcanprint.it
info@youcanprint.it
Facebook: facebook.com/youcanprint.it
Twitter: twitter.com/youcanprintit

INDEX

Preface

The present study, well documented from the Dr. Cinzia RANDAZZO, offers not only one rise of reflection for further fields of search, correlated always to the theme of the education, but also a specific elucidation to a theme, that of the education, that, in the primitive community christian, it was strongly felt both from the simple people and from those people whom "*educators*" was considered. Strong it was in fact since the beginning of the history of the church the worry to educate the young people, for which the role of the family and of the community christian was fundamental, as it was also it the Gospel, pivot around which rotate both the Christian education and that human, whose models were visible in the life that conduct the Christian wise men.

Under this aspect this study seems pertinent to to make again present in the today the sense that gave to the education our first Christians, to which every man of good will has called to put himself as in front of a mirror.

Rome, 27-11-2014

Prof. Anthony CASTELLANO
(Ordinary teacher of
christology to the UPS)

Introduction

The idea to turn a particular attention to the juvenile education is dictated by the fact that it exists one proliferated entourage of studies related to such matter especially in our epoch, while instead it not there are specific studies circumscribed to the period subapostolic.

If it is true that a small monograph exists on the education to the origins of the Christianity,[1] it go away itself, for content, from the title, having covered, under the diction "*to the origins of the Christianity*" the whole arc of time that extends him from the real origin of the Christianity until the included the advent of the monastic orders, illustrating to great lines the to unfold himself of the pedagogic tendencies both in field pagan that Christian.

It seems opportune to such point that a return to the origins of the Christianity is of fundamental importance above all for to deepen the concept of education since his to be born, as it emerges from a careful reading of the texts of the apostolic fathers; concept that will be then by to spread in our young people today.

With this intent we propose there to do an analysis detailed of the operas of the apostolic fathers, dated among the end of the 1 century d.C. and the halves of the second, conscious that it is not possible to try to educate the young people without to know their thought, because it is from there that the new Christian education is born, founded upon the fear of God.

---

[1] H. von SCHUBERT (trad. it. di G. SANNA), *Istruzione ed educazione alle origini del cristianesimo*, Venezia 1929.

1. The educational role of the parents and of the adults

1.1. *The concept of education*

1.1.1. Circular condition

Fundamental condition without which the education of the young people is not possible is the presence of the small children: "*The great cannot be without the small and the small without the great*".[2] Clemente Romano shows that the adult cannot impart the education to the small if these miss and vice versa. The activity of the to educate is possible graces to the presence of the educator (wise adult) and the educate (small young, child), because if it misses one of the two such exercise it is void.

Under this aspect the exercise of the education is reversing because it can lose its effectiveness when one of the two parts misses. Such exercise is not only reversing but also circular, in how much the education is founded upon the communication among the two interlocutors (educating and educate). In this communication the connection emerges among the two subjects: "*in all the things there is some connection and in this the utility*".[3] Because there is the education the educating one, according to Clemente, it has the obligation to establish a communicative circularity with he who it is in procinto to educate because among the two there is connection and dialogue interaction. The image that Clemente uses for making to notice this is that of the body and of his limbs:

---

[2] CLEMENTE ROMANO, *Epistola ai Corinti* 37,4. Ed. crit. F.X. FUNK-K. BIHLMEYER-M. WHITTAKER, *Die Apostolischen Väter. Griechisch-deutsche Parallelausgabe*, 120. Trad. di A. QUACQUARELLI, *I Padri Apostolici*, p. 74.

[3] CLEMENTE ROMANO, *Epistola ai Corinti* 37,4. Ed. crit. F.X. FUNK-K. BIHLMEYER-M. WHITTAKER, *Die Apostolischen Väter. Griechisch-deutsche Parallelausgabe*, 120. Trad. di A. QUACQUARELLI, *I Padri Apostolici*, p. 74.

The head cannot be without the feet, neither the feet without the head. The smallest parts of our body are necessary and useful to the whole body; but all cohabit and they have an only subordination to save the whole body.[4]

This educational circularity between the drawer (educator) and the receptor (educated) is appanage of that educational circularity that is established between Father and Child in Saturday *protological* yet before of the creation; both the circularity are finalized to the salvation: the first one because it is cause of the creation, that is of the leaving of the darkness and the to be revealed some light, the second because it is at the base of the salvation of the educate one, in how much he who are educated is formed to entirely desire the Good in all the things, so that in this walk of progressive similarity to God, he saves himself. Under this aspect he who are educated to know himself care his soul to reach the eternal salvation.

1.1.2. Virtual conditions

Because it becomes itself some good educators it is necessary to flee the street of the death, avoiding to make the acts followings:

— to persecute the good person:
Persecutor (διῶκται) of the good person (.). From them it is distant the calm and the patience; they are lovers of the vain things, (.) killers of their children.[5]

---

[4] CLEMENTE ROMANO, *Epistola ai Corinti* 37,5. Ed. crit. F.X. FUNK-K. BIHLMEYER-M. WHITTAKER, *Die Apostolischen Väter. Griechisch-deutsche Parallelausgabe*, 120. Trad. di A. QUACQUARELLI, *I Padri Apostolici*, p. 74.

[5] *Didachè* V,2. Ed. crit. F.X. FUNK-K. BIHLMEYER-M. WHITTAKER, *Die Apostolischen Väter. Griechisch-deutsche Parallelausgabe*, 120. Trad. di A. QUACQUARELLI, *I Padri Apostolici*, p. 33.

The persecutor are grasped from a spirit of torment, whose map of litmus mirrors itself in that group of demons that impute to Christ the cause of their torment, while instead are theirs the carriers of such uneasiness, because their spirit is not turned toward the supernal things (Mt 8,28 -29).

These spirits are already in prey to the torment, because direct to satisfy their negative impulses that are contrary to those that are tensed to the search of the Truth. Beginning from such picture the persecutor are those people who are strongly bound by this horrible carnal thirst of nuisance and torment because their mind is not in peace with God, in how much is away from Him, for which these are denominated *"children's killers."* The true educator is instead he who is mild and serene as Christ, which he doesn't allow to torment, because its spirit is permanently in tuning with that of his Father: *"You take my yoke above of you and learned by me, that am mild and humble of heart, and you will find comfort for your souls"* (Mt 11,29).

     - To hate the truth. For the author of the *Didachè* it is not a good educator he who it hates the Truth:

> Odiatori of the Truth (.). From them it is distant
> the calm and the patience; they are lovers of the
> vain things (.); children's killers.[6]

He who hate the Truth it follows the negative tendencies of the meat that make him slave of his own carnal instincts and therefore subdued to their desires. Under this aspect the denial of if same is the way main to follow the Truth: *"Who loves his father or her mother more than me it is not worthy of me; who loves his child or her*

---

[6] *Didachè* V,2. Ed. crit. F.X. FUNK-K. BIHLMEYER-M. WHITTAKER, *Die Apostolischen Väter. Griechisch-deutsche Parallelausgabe*, 10. Trad. di A. QUACQUARELLI, *I Padri Apostolici*, p. 33.

daughter more than me it is not worthy of me" (Mt 10,37).

- To love the lie: "*lovers of the lie (.) from them it is distant the calm and the patience (.) children's killers*".[7] Those people who follow the lie are compared to Adamo and Eva that have followed the word of the snake that before Eva has deceived and then Adamo (Gen 2 -3).
- To ignore the prize of the justice:
unaware of the prize of the justice (.). From them it is distant the calm and the patience; they are lovers of the vain things, avid of the reward, merciless with the poor man, intolerant with whom is oppressed, not thankful toward who has created them; children's killers.[8]

The author of the *Didachè* takes back the thought of Paul, for which to every Christian the assignment impends to race for coming to take the prize of the justice on the model of the athletes that they are intents to race to receive the final prize in the stadium (1Cor 9,24 -25).

The true educators of the faith have the assignment to hold always the eyes fixed to the justice of God, to get ready for to educate the children with perseverance in the faith in Christ.

- Not to adhere to the good and to the right judgment: "*not adherent to the good neither to the right judgment*".[9] For the author of the *Didachè* the

---

[7] *Didachè* V,2. Ed. crit. F.X. FUNK-K. BIHLMEYER-M. WHITTAKER, *Die Apostolischen Väter. Griechisch-deutsche Parallelausgabe*, 10. Trad. di A. QUACQUARELLI, *I Padri Apostolici*, p. 33.

[8] *Didachè* V,2. Ed. crit. F.X. FUNK-K. BIHLMEYER-M. WHITTAKER, *Die Apostolischen Väter. Griechisch-deutsche Parallelausgabe*, 10. Trad. di A. QUACQUARELLI, *I Padri Apostolici*, p. 33.

[9] *Didachè* V,2. Ed. crit. F.X. FUNK-K. BIHLMEYER-M. WHITTAKER, *Die Apostolischen Väter. Griechisch-deutsche Parallelausgabe*, 10. Trad. di A.

Christians are called to seek the Good and to rightly judge. From the Christian there is needed a period of preparation and of constancy in the faith, on the track of the first letter of Paul to the Cor 9,27. The progressive walk of the Christian is turned not to the return, that is in the condition in which he had departed, but to a superior aim, so that becomes similar to the Father.

− To watch over the evil. Every Christian educator knows that during the walk the obligation impends to watch over for not to fall in temptation, that is not to return in the situation in which he had departed, in line with how much Jesus has told his disciples (Mt 26,40-41). The motives that are at the base of such deviant attitudes are the followings:

− the love for the corruptible things

− the lack of the calm and of the patience

− the lack of the fear of God, in how much it misses the feeling of the thankfulness toward God that has created them:

From them it is distant the calm and the patience; they are lovers of the vain things, avid of the reward, merciless with the poor man, intolerant with whom is oppressed, not thankful toward who has created them; children's killers, destroyers of the creature of God, regardless of the pauper .[10]

QUACQUARELLI, *I Padri Apostolici,* p. 33.

[10] *Didachè* V,2. Ed. crit. F.X. FUNK-K. BIHLMEYER-M. WHITTAKER, *Die Apostolischen Väter. Griechisch-deutsche Parallelausgabe,* 10. Trad. di A. QUACQUARELLI, *I Padri Apostolici,* p. 33.

1.2. *Education to the justice*

1.2.1. Conditions

The lack of anger, for the *Shepherd* of Erma, it is another condition because the child is educated:

> You Erma not to be angry with your children neither to skip your sister because is purified from their sins of before. They will educate themselves with a correct address if you won't bring them resentment. The resentment produces the death.[11]

The lack of the resentment, that is of the grudge or of the continuous hate, it allows the parent to educate his child second "*justice.*"[12] Here Erma refers himself to the justice of Christ, intending with this not to give to the child what is up to (the due one) him, but to educate the child following the optics of the conversion of the heart in function of the purification of the sins committed by the children, because is established between parents and children a circularity educational based on the love (pardon) and not on the grudge. Under this aspect to the child is imparted a education based on the reconciliation with God that makes lever or it has its pivot on the justice, that is on the conversion of the heart that allows the pardon and therefore to the purification of the sins.

---

[11] ERMA, *Pastore, Visione* 2,7,1. Ed. crit. F.X. FUNK-K. BIHLMEYER-M. WHITTAKER, *Die Apostolischen Väter. Griechisch-deutsche Parallelausgabe*, 340. Trad. di A. QUACQUARELLI, *I Padri Apostolici*, 248.

[12] ERMA, *Pastore, Visione* 2,7,1.3.4. Ed. crit. F.X. FUNK-K. BIHLMEYER-M. WHITTAKER, *Die Apostolischen Väter. Griechisch-deutsche Parallelausgabe*, 340. Trad. di A. QUACQUARELLI, *I Padri Apostolici*, pp. 248-249.

1.2.2. Effects

According to the author of the *Didachè* it are reputed *"children's killers"* the parents that follow the street of the death: *"The street of the death is this. Indeed it is bad and full of curse: homicides (...) 2. Persecutor of the good (...) children's killers"*.[13] The parent that kills the child is sower of death because he not consider the child to be a creature of God: *"Destroyers of the creature of God"*.[14] The author of the *Didachè* explains that the killers of the children are that circle of parents that consider the child a object and subdued to their will. This way to involve itself injures, in line with the commandment of God *"not to kill"* (Deut 5,17), the dignity of the child, of the same parents and of the same God that has created them both. In line with the *"principle"* of Gen 1, all the living beings are creatures of God, because moulded by the hands of the same God that has blown in the nostrils the vital puff, that is a particle of his spirit.

Under this aspect the parents are kept not to consider the children *"his ownership"*, but *"God's ownership"* as themselves, in how much all the living beings are children of the same God that have created them.

Another form of moral deviance is the rebellion of the young people against the old people: *"So rebelled himself (.) the young people against the old people."*.[15]

---

[13] *Didachè* V,1.2. Ed. crit. F.X. FUNK-K. BIHLMEYER-M. WHITTAKER, *Die Apostolischen Väter. Griechisch-deutsche Parallelausgabe*, 10. Trad. di A. QUACQUARELLI, *I Padri Apostolici*, pp. 32-33.

[14] *Didachè* V,2. Ed. crit. F.X. FUNK-K. BIHLMEYER-M. WHITTAKER, *Die Apostolischen Väter. Griechisch-deutsche Parallelausgabe*, 10. Trad. di A. QUACQUARELLI, *I Padri Apostolici*, p. 33.

[15] CLEMENTE ROMANO, *Epistola ai Corinti* 3,3. Ed. crit. F.X. FUNK-K. BIHLMEYER-M. WHITTAKER, *Die Apostolischen Väter. Griechisch-deutsche Parallelausgabe*, 82. Trad. di A. QUACQUARELLI, *I Padri Apostolici*, 51.

According to Clemente Romano such form of rebellion is caused by the fact that the young people have abandoned the fear of God, in how much they don't behave according to the commandments of the Lord, because they follow the passions of their wicked heart:

> For this it are gotten away the justice and the peace, in how much each has abandoned the fear of God and he has darkened his faith; it not walk according to the divine commandments, it doesn't behave as it is worthwhile to Christ, but it proceeds according to the passions of his wicked heart.[16]

The rebellion of the young people is imputable, according to Clemente Romano, to the progressive abandon of the young people from the fear of God, that is by to render to God respect, reverence and attention as to a friend.

This form of overcoming to God, that it manifests itself in the rebellion of the young people against all of this that God has created, - and therefore also against the old people – it is daughter of the jealousy, cause, for Clemente, of the eternal death.[17] In Clemente recurs the thought of Sap 2,24 that it will be taken again in Rm 5,12:

> Then, as because of an only man the sin has entered in the world and with the sin the death, so also the death has reached all the men, because all have sinned.

---

[16] CLEMENTE ROMANO, *Epistola ai Corinti* 3,4. Ed. crit. F.X. FUNK-K. BIHLMEYER-M. WHITTAKER, *Die Apostolischen Väter. Griechisch-deutsche Parallelausgabe*, 82-84. Trad. di A. QUACQUARELLI, *I Padri Apostolici*, p. 51.

[17] CLEMENTE ROMANO, *Epistola ai Corinti* 3,4. Ed. crit. F.X. FUNK-K. BIHLMEYER-M. WHITTAKER, *Die Apostolischen Väter. Griechisch-deutsche Parallelausgabe*, Tübingen 1992, 82-84. Trad. di A. QUACQUARELLI, *I Padri Apostolici*, 51.

Besides the author of the *Didachè* exhorts the adults to abstain from contaminate the boys: "*Not to contaminate (παιδοφθορήσεις) the boys*".[18] The verb παιδοφθορεῖν, coming from παῖς (boy) + φθείρω (to ruin),[19] it is employed by the author of the *Didaché* to show that the adults have the assignment not to contaminate the boys, that is not to make to turn their desires entirely toward the things of the earth that are corruptible. It emerges the sense of the apostle Paul of the corruption of the terrestrial life, because all this that belongs of the terrestrial life is stamped to the transient, to the temporary (1 Cor 9,25) and finalized to the consumption of the things and to their destruction (Col 2,22) and therefore not to the eternal values. The author of the *Didachè*, in line with the thought of the apostle Paul, expresses the intention to avoid that the boys dot limitedly on their character of creature, because their present reality is turned to the dissolution, to the death that is proper of this world. It plays again the antithesis of the apostle Paul between terrestrial corruptibility and celestial incorruptibility (Rm 2,7); for this motive every adult is kept to direct the boys toward the gifts of the Spirit because these are incorruptible, so that, watering himself to such gifts, they can become incorruptible, already enjoying on the earth the true eternal fruits of the Spirit.

Under this aspect the adults have the assignment to address the boys to make participate them some divine life, so that doesn't stay trapped in the jail of the terrestrial life from which it bud the corruptible goods because of the lust

---

[18] *Didaché* 2,2. Ed. crit. F.X. FUNK-K. BIHLMEYER-M. WHITTAKER, *Die Apostolischen Väter. Griechisch-deutsche Parallelausgabe*, Tübingen 1992, 6. Trad. di A. QUACQUARELLI, *I Padri Apostolici*, Roma 2000, 30.

[19] T. HOLTZ, *Φθείρω*, in H. BALZ-G. SCHNEIDER, *Dizionario esegetico del Nuovo Testamento*, vol. II, Brescia 1998, 1788-1792.

(2Pt 1,4).

1.3. *Education to the moderation and to the dignity*

Clemente Romano turns to the Corintis his gratifying appeal to have been faithful to the law of the Lord, in how much they have also instilled in the young people the sense of the moderation and of the dignity: *"You exhorted the young people to think (νοεῖν) things moderate (μέτρια) and worthy (σεμνὰ)"*.[20] The persons responsible of the community of Corinto are lavished to turn the mind of the young verse the correct equilibrium with the purpose to direct their thought toward the things that don't exceed or don't decrease the correct measure of all the things. Concrete it has been their will to make moderate the mind of the young people, so that knows to measure all the things with correct measure and to give to every thing the correct due, that is what competes him without excesses and neither regresses. They have implemented in the mind of the young people the virtue of the moderation, through which they have the tendency to give to every thing what it is her due.

Further to direct the mind of the young people toward the virtue of the moderation the persons responsible are alternated to haul the thought of the young people toward worthy things and toward things that God likes and that don't offend the modesty and that don't injure the sense of the good course of the civil way of living; springing sense from the image of God that is placed in every man. The persons responsible of the community are directed to give to the young theoretical examples stamped to the

---

[20] CLEMENTE ROMANO, *ai Corinti* 1,3. Ed. crit. F.X. FUNK-K. BIHLMEYER-M. WHITTAKER, *Die Apostolischen Väter. Griechisch-deutsche Parallelausgabe*, 80. Trad. di A. QUACQUARELLI, *I Padri Apostolici*, 50.

dignity; examples that have the finality to orchestrate the thought of the young people toward things that build the humanity according to the project of salvation of God, going away them so from that all that unhealthy thoughts that drag them toward unbridled and messy impulses that inevitably conduct them toward the perdition and therefore toward the breakup of the them same to be psico-physical and not toward the unity of this them same to be. It resorts in the letter to the Corintis the same accent of exhortation, turned to the young people, of the letter to Tito. In 2,6 Paul turns him to Tito because he exhorts the young people to *"to be judicious"* (Tt 2,6): "*It still exhorts the more young people to be judicious (σωφρονεῖν)* " (Tt 2,6). In the letter to Tito such oral expression is index of moderation[21]; virtue that it is lived by those people who choose to live an intense rational life, "*that it consists in the refusal of worldly greeds.*"[22] For the adults impends the obligation to render the young people judicious, giving them a suitable formation psico-physics and virtual that makes them worthy of to be simple and reserved, in such way that their reserve both appanage of the dignity of God that has created the man simple and moderate, because is not pompous and affected in his thoughts. The young people are exhorted not to pompously exalt their qualities to loss of the others, but to become, in front of the others, living mirror of the reserved and judicious simplicity of God, where the word is not empty and end to herself as in the charlatan, to the contrary it is united to the action, for which the two things are not untied but united, on the model of

---

[21] Cfr. D. ZELLER, σώφρων, in H. BALZ – G. SCHNEIDER, *Dizionario Esegetico del Nuovo Testamento*, vol. 2, col. 1558.

[22] *Ibidem*

God that speaks few and it completes great things: "*God said: «it is the light», and the light was*" (Gen 1,1).

1.4. *Education to the fear of God*
1.4.1. Conditions

Clemente Romano exhorts the Corintis to educate the young people to the fear of God: "*We educate (παιδεύωμεν) the young people to the fear (φόβου) of God.*".[23] Clemente Romano, for to wake up in the young people the sense of the attention and of the respect toward God, uses the verb παιδεύειν that in the Greek antiquity it designated

> the education and the care of the little boy that growing will enter to belong to the world of the adults and it has therefore need of guide, teaching, education and also of a certain constraint, that is of the discipline and also of the punishment.[24]

Such form verbal comes from παιδεία, with which term is indicated "*the walk that the education and the formation must cross and it are also the destination to reach*".[25] The term παιδεία it implicates the experience and the admonishment as condition for the educator, initials and essential to drive the little boy through the teaching of his fundamental notions. At the base of all this the educator aims at to "*to make to hate what is detestable and to love*

---

[23] CLEMENTE ROMANO, *Epistola ai Corinti* 21,6. Ed. crit. F.X. FUNK-K. BIHLMEYER-M. WHITTAKER, *Die Apostolischen Väter. Griechisch-deutsche Parallelausgabe*, 104. Trad. di A. QUACQUARELLI, *I Padri Apostolici*, p. 64.

[24] G. BERTRAM, παιδεύω, in G. KITTEL-G. FRIEDRICH, *Grande Lessico del Nuovo Testamento*, vol. IX, col. 106.

[25] *Ibidem*

what is agreeable.".[26] It belongs to the sphere of the Truth and of the top Well what it is agreeable, for which the educator aims to cultivate the virtues of the Spirit because the young people can be educated according to his teaching.

Returning to the letter to the Corintis to the persons responsible impends the obligation not only to be of the good and brave educators, from which shines a good behavior of life through but also of the good instructors, because can instruct the young people to the true *παιδεία*, that is to the immortal virtues of the Spirit, warning himself, in line with the Aristotelian thought, against the vain tendencies of the meat.[27]

Under this aspect the exhortation to the education (paideia) implicates for the educators from a side their behavior of life that becomes exemplary to the young one because is lived according to the divine model of the true education that in itself it is immortal and divine[28] and from the other the teaching of the same, through the oral form of the admonishment. To the educator therefore competes the assignment to be a person who has really fear of God, from the moment that the education of the young people is to be finalized to the fear of God.

The fear of God is one of the virtues that conducts the man to have reverence, attention and respect toward God[29], to consider him as a friend for which the adults, responsible of the community of Corinto, is kept to be the

---

[26] PLATONE, Leggi 2,653 c.

[27] ARISTOTELE, *Etica nicomachea* 1336b23.

[28] Vedi SOCRATE in PLATONE, *Clit.* 407a

[29] Cfr. C. RANDAZZO, *La teologia del timore di Dio agli esordi del cristianesimo*, Tricase 2014.

more wise than the community because only these are designate, according to the thought ancient of Socrate, to educate the young people to the fear of God: *"the more wise educates to the fear of God and to the regal dignity"*.[30]

Beginning from such picture, on the base of his wisdom and his true behavior lived according to the virtue of the fear of God, the adults of the community of Corinto were primarily designated to this task and consequently therefore to teach such virtue, hocking himself together with the young people to complete such formative walk. The young people were educated to the fear of God that is not the simple knowledge of God, in how much, taking back the words of the anonymous author of the *to Diogneto*, the knowledge without the love it inflates while the love for the true life edify.[31] Her simple knowledge of God without the love for him it doesn't edify because the man becomes aware of to know many things but not carry fruit, in how much he doesn't love the true life.[32]

Under this aspect the young people are not only educated to know God, but to love him in manner by have him always near to render him part integral of his own life, without which the man would lose the sense of the true life and therefore his same image of man tense to desire the supernal things. In this way in Clemente it plays again the thought of the to *Diogneto* 12,6-7, because the educator not only has the assignment to make to know the virtue of the

---

[30] Ps. PLATONE, *Alcibiade* 1,121e-122a

[31] *A Diogneto* 12,5. Ed. Crit. F.X. FUNK-K. BIHLMEYER-M. WHITTAKER, *Die Apostolischen Väter. Griechisch-deutsche Parallelausgabe*, 322. Trad. di E. NORELLI, *A Diogneto*, Milano 1991, 130.

[32] *A Diogneto* 12,6. Ed. crit. F.X. FUNK-K. BIHLMEYER-M. WHITTAKER, *Die Apostolischen Väter. Griechisch-deutsche Parallelausgabe*, 322. Trad. di E. NORELLI, *A Diogneto*, Milano 1991, p. 130

fear of God but to arouse in him the desire to love God, to welcome him in his heart, so that through the knowledge, united to the virtue of the fear of God, the young can reach to the true knowledge of God and therefore to love the true life. Particularly Policarpo specifies that the women also have the assignment to educate their children: "*Besides that your women (...) the children educate in the fear of God.*".[33] The exhortation of Policarpo is turned to the women that have the duty to educate the children, showing so that the woman has integral part as the man in the education of the children. It is rediscovered so the feminine role in the education of the children; role that in the Jewish tradition and in the thought of the apostle Paul was attributed only to the Father.[34]

Under this aspect the woman assumes for Policarpo an active role in the education of the children to the fear of God. According to Policarpo the woman is not excluded by the education of the children, but she has integral part in this function because, as the man, has been created to image of God. In strength of this equal regal dignity that has been given by God to the woman; dignity founded to the origins of the world, Policarpo infers this thought attributing the same educational function to the woman that, for tradition, it belonged to the man.

Other condition because the parent can establish a correct educational circularity with the child it is the teaching of the fear of God: "*Not to send away the hand from your child and from your daughter, but from the*

---

³³ POLICARPO, *ai Filippesi* 4,2.   Ed. crit. F.X. FUNK-K. BIHLMEYER-M. WHITTAKER, *Die Apostolischen Väter. Griechisch-deutsche Parallelausgabe*, 248. Trad. di A. QUACQUARELLI, *I Padri Apostolici*, 155.

³⁴ G. BERTRAM, παιδεύω, in G. KITTEL-G. FRIEDRICH, *Grande Lessico del Nuovo Testamento*, vol. IX, col. 129. Vedi anche Ef 6,4.

infancy you will teach them the fear (φόβον) of God.".[35] At the base of the education of the child there is the education or better the knowledge of the fear of God from part of the parents. To them competes the obligation to furnish to the child the following instructions around the virtue of the fear of God:

- God's fear in positive sense. It is not the fear of God but the respectful reservedness, or better the respect that who God desires it turns verse of him.

> – The person who has fear of God has the obligation to have a good behaviour of God, because he loves him and desires him above all the things.
>
> – In whatever circumstance of the daily life the person who has fear of God is called to abandon himself in the hands of God, confident of his intervention in his favor and of his salvation and protection.
>
> – To the person who has fear of God impends the duty to be subdued to God and to turn to him the due respect and the due reverence.

1.5. *Mutual education to the insignia of the temperance*

Other condition, according to the *Shepherd* of Erma, because every responsible of community can become a good educator it is the mutual education, imparted according to the virtue of the temperance:

> This intemperance is harmful for you that you
> possess and not dates to the paupers (.) 6. You

---

[35] Ps. BARNABA, *Epistola* 19,5. Ed. crit. F.X. FUNK-K. BIHLMEYER-M. WHITTAKER, *Die Apostolischen Väter. Griechisch-deutsche Parallelausgabe*, 70. Trad. di A. QUACQUARELLI, *I Padri Apostolici*, 212.

watch out you that you boast you of your wealth that the paupers are never afflicted and their complaint doesn't climb to the Lord. With your goods is not closed the door of the tower 7. I tell you that you are the heads of the church and you occupy the first places: you don't do you similar to the wizards. The wizards bring their filters in the little vases, you bring your filter, the poison, in the heart. 8. You are hardened and you don't want to purify you, to melt your feeling in the pure heart to get mercy from the great king (.). 10. How can you educate the chosen of God, if you are not you educated? Educate you, therefore, each other and you live in peace because I, to the presence of the Father, am happy to speak of all of you. [36]

The church, symbolized as an elderly woman, it exhorts the heads of the church to reciprocally educate himself to the virtue of the temperance - virtue that consists in the to give to the paupers what is due for the necessary food and maintenance – in how much such education mutual carry to live in the peace and not in the discord. Here the church exhorts the heads of the church not to multiply their wealths and their material well-being to loss of the increasing poverty of the paupers, victims of the abuse and of the abandonment from part of the rich. The church exhorts to the charity (love) toward the needy; love that achieves from the virtue of the temperance, according to which the man hocks himself to give to the pauper how much to him is necessary, with the remuneration not to

[36] ERMA, *Pastore,Vis.* 3,17,4.6.7.8.10. Ed. crit. F.X. FUNK-K. BIHLMEYER-M. WHITTAKER, *Die Apostolischen Väter. Griechisch-deutsche Parallelausgabe*, 358-360. Trad. di A. QUACQUARELLI, *I Padri Apostolici,* pp. 258-259.

increase his own wealths. It's up to, according to Erma, to the heads of the church the mutual education to such virtue, from the moment that they excel in goods and possessions of material order.

The virtue of the intemperance, to which they are subject, derives from their sclerocardia and it can be removed if their heart is purified: *"You are hardened and you don't want to purify you, to melt your feeling in the pure heart to get mercy from the great King"*.[37] The exhortation of Erma traces that of Jesus, for which it is easier than the camel pass for the eye of a needle that a rich to give his own goods to the poor men (Mt 19,24).

Beginning from such picture the heads of the church, according to Erma, they are called to purify their heart to get mercy from God, with the purpose to desire the true life, that is the Truth and not the corruptible (material wealths) things, in manner from to be true educators on the earth: *"As you can educate the chosen of God, if you not are educated?"*.[38] For Erma therefore it impends to the heads of the church the obligation to purify their heart from the intemperance to live in peace, becoming concrete educators of the Truth.

2. The educational model for the young people

2.1. *The educational model of Christ*

Clemente Romano quotes the scriptural testimonium of Is 53,1 applying the appellative of little boy to Christ: "

---

[37] ERMA, *Pastore, Vis.* 3,17,8-9. Ed. crit. F.X. FUNK-K. BIHLMEYER-M. WHITTAKER, *Die Apostolischen Väter. Griechisch-deutsche Parallelausgabe*, 360. Trad. di A. QUACQUARELLI, *I Padri Apostolici*, 258-259.

[38] ERMA, *Pastore, Vis.* 3,17,9,10. Ed. crit. F.X. FUNK-K. BIHLMEYER-M. WHITTAKER, *Die Apostolischen Väter. Griechisch-deutsche Parallelausgabe*, 360. Trad. di A. QUACQUARELLI, *I Padri Apostolici,* p. 259.

He is as a little boy, as a root in the thirsty earth; it has neither appearance nor glory."[39] He shows to his community that, to the same standard of a little boy that is obedient to the orders of the Father in how much it subdues himself to his will, Christ has come in the world not in the boldness and in the pride, but in the humility:

> Christ is of the humble, not of whom raises himself on his flock. 2. The scepter of the majesty of God, the Lord Jesus Christ, didn't come in the din of the boldness and of the pride, - and he would have been able - but in the humility of heart as the Spirit Saint had to say of him.[40]

The image of the root, taken back by Isaia, it is meaningful in order to the humility of heart. With this image Clemente wants to point out that the humility of heart of Christ is comparable to the root, because the root is hidden in the earth, it doesn't make herself see also supporting the earth. To the same standard of the root Christ doesn't show and doesn't make to see his beautiful qualities, but it supports the world, also not showing such qualities. He supports the world in how much it bears on himself the sins of the whole humanity and for this reason it hides the beauty of his face, appearing disfigured: "*We saw him, it didn't have a beautiful appearance, but its aspect was despicable, away from the aspect of the men.*"[41]

---

[39] CLEMENTE ROMANO, *Epistola ai Corinti* 16,3. Ed. crit. F.X. FUNK-K. BIHLMEYER-M. WHITTAKER, *Die Apostolischen Väter. Griechisch-deutsche Parallelausgabe*, p. 96. Trad. di A. QUACQUARELLI, *I Padri Apostolici*, p. 59.

[40] CLEMENTE ROMANO, *Epistola ai Corinti* 16,1-2. Ed. crit. F.X. FUNK-K. BIHLMEYER-M. WHITTAKER, *Die Apostolischen Väter. Griechisch-deutsche Parallelausgabe*, p. 96. Trad. di A. QUACQUARELLI, *I Padri Apostolici*, p. 59.

[41] CLEMENTE ROMANO, *Epistola ai Corinti* 16,3. Ed. crit. F.X. FUNK-K. BIHLMEYER-M. WHITTAKER, *Die Apostolischen Väter. Griechisch-deutsche*

To the same standard of the root, Clemente Romano continues, also the afflicted man and without honour it hides his face: "*As the man that is in the hits and in the suffering and that he knows to bear the affliction because it hides his face, it was not honoured and calculated*".[42]

Under this aspect, Clemente Romano, recalling himself to the image of the root that is without face in how much symbol of the humility, to the same standard of a struck man, it numbers the virtue of the humility of heart to educational model for the community and for the same young people.

The educational model that Clemente proposes to his community is founded on the humility, that is that particular predisposition of heart turned to bear the other people's lacks and to suffer for these, to the same standard of Christ that "*carry our sins and it suffers for us, and we have considered that was in the suffering, in the affliction and in the maltreatment*".[43] In the suffering and in the humility the man redeems himself, to the same standard of Jesus, because "*in the humiliation its sentence was removed*".[44] The sacrifices are numbered by Clemente Romano as remedy salutary for the soul sinner, because thanks to these the Lord gives to this "*a long posterity*": "*If you make sacrifices for the sin, your soul she will see a*

Parallelausgabe, p. 96. Trad. di A. QUACQUARELLI, *I Padri Apostolici*, p. 59.

[42] CLEMENTE ROMANO, *Epistola ai Corinti* 16,3. Ed. crit. F.X. FUNK-K. BIHLMEYER-M. WHITTAKER, *Die Apostolischen Väter. Griechisch-deutsche Parallelausgabe*, p. 96. Trad. di A. QUACQUARELLI, *I Padri Apostolici*, p. 59.

[43] CLEMENTE ROMANO, *Epistola ai Corinti* 16,4. Ed. crit. F.X. FUNK-K. BIHLMEYER-M. WHITTAKER, *Die Apostolischen Väter. Griechisch-deutsche Parallelausgabe*, p. 96. Trad. di A. QUACQUARELLI, *I Padri Apostolici*, p. 59.

[44] CLEMENTE ROMANO, *Epistola ai Corinti* 16,7. Ed. crit. F.X. FUNK-K. BIHLMEYER-M. WHITTAKER, *Die Apostolischen Väter. Griechisch-deutsche Parallelausgabe*, p. 98. Trad. di A. QUACQUARELLI, *I Padri Apostolici*, p. 60.

long posterity".[45] Clemente Romano exhorts the children to become participate of the education in Christ; education that a child can receive if he learns to be living torch of the same humility and the same love that Christ has lived for us, powerful ramparts of true education and of salvation near God: *"Our children participate of the education in Christ; learns what can the humility and the love near the Lord"*.[46]

Clemente Romano specifies that the educational model for the children has its base in the humility and in the love: from the union of both the virtues the child would participate of the same education of Christ; education that the Father has given to the Child yet before of the creation and that he has made concrete in his tallest form in the Saturday of Easter (soteriological), where the Child in the humility of the cross has given himself for the salvation of the humanity. It is not even excluded by the educational model of Christ the irreproachability, to which every youth can conform himself if it approaches itself the more possible to the purity and it set itself a brake in front of every form of badly: *"Equally the young people are faultless in everything, considering the purity and braking himself before to every evil"*.[47]

According to Policarpo the conditions for becoming faultless they are the purity and the to set brake in front of

[45] CLEMENTE ROMANO, *Epistola ai Corinti* 16,11. Ed. crit. F.X. FUNK-K. BIHLMEYER-M. WHITTAKER, *Die Apostolischen Väter. Griechisch-deutsche Parallelausgabe*, p. 98. Trad. di A. QUACQUARELLI, *I Padri Apostolici*, p. 60.

[46] CLEMENTE ROMANO, *Epistola ai Corinti* 21,8. Ed. Crit. F.X. FUNK-K. BIHLMEYER-M. WHITTAKER, *Die Apostolischen Väter. Griechisch-deutsche Parallelausgabe*, 106. Trad. di A. QUACQUARELLI, *I Padri Apostolici*, 64.

[47] POLICARPO, *ai Filippesi* 5,3. Ed. crit. F.X. FUNK-K. BIHLMEYER-M. WHITTAKER, *Die Apostolischen Väter. Griechisch-deutsche Parallelausgabe*, p. 248. Trad. di A. QUACQUARELLI, *I Padri Apostolici*, p. 156

every evil. Policarpo shows in the irreproachability the educational model of Christ for the young people, because same Christ during his life maintained himself free from every form of material and moral contamination, in how much it was really him the healer of all the evil. To the eyes of Christ, according to the pseudo-Clemente, all the men are called children: *"As a father he called us children and it saved us while we were for losing us"*.[48]

The pseudo-Clemente, giving the appellative of father to Christ and connecting the salvation to the human progeny, he wants to make to realize to his community that Christ has loved the man, that were in the orgy of the corruptible goods, because he has him turned to desire those eternal:

> blind of mind we adored stones, woods, gold, silver and bronze, operas of men. All of our life was death. We were surrounded by the darkness and full of so much obscurity in the eyes. For his to want we repurchased the sight breaking the haze that wound us [49]

Thanks to the love of salvation of Christ and to his great mercy the man has been able to turn the look to the incorruptible goods: *"It had mercy of us and moved to pity it saved us"*.[50] Before of the salvation and therefore before of a good re-education to the eternal life there is the affliction, because every man suffers in reason of the

---

[48] Ps. CLEMENTE, *Omelia* 1,4. Ed. crit. F.X. FUNK-K. BIHLMEYER-M. WHITTAKER, *Die Apostolischen Väter. Griechisch-deutsche Parallelausgabe*, p. 154. Trad. di A. QUACQUARELLI, *I Padri Apostolici*, p. 221.

[49] Ps. CLEMENTE, *Omelia* 1,6. Ed. crit. F.X. FUNK-K. BIHLMEYER-M. WHITTAKER, *Die Apostolischen Väter. Griechisch-deutsche Parallelausgabe*, p. 154. Trad. di A. QUACQUARELLI, *I Padri Apostolici*, p. 221.

[50] Ps. CLEMENTE, *Omelia* 1,7. Ed. crit. F.X. FUNK-K. BIHLMEYER-M. WHITTAKER, *Die Apostolischen Väter. Griechisch-deutsche Parallelausgabe*, p. 154. Trad. di A. QUACQUARELLI, *I Padri Apostolici*, pp. 303-304.

gravity of his own actions:

> When it are afflicted from every tribulation
> then are delivered to me for a good re-
> education (...) justly each has everything
> suffered according to his own actions.[51]

Erma specifies that those people whom operated badly are victims of different punishments and torments, which are poured again on the man sinner on the base of his actions:

> He (the angel of the punishment) takes those
> that have erred away from God walking in the
> street of the passions and of the pleasures of
> this world and he punish them, as each has
> deserved, with different atrocious
> punishments.[52]

Beginning from such picture the tests of the life are due, according to Erma, to the dissolute actions of those people that have favored the pleasures and the passions:

> the various tests and punishments are the tests
> of the life. Some are punished with illnesses,
> others with deprivations, others with various
> illnesses, others with every misfortune; finally
> others are offended from unworthy and they
> suffer a lot other evil. 5. Many uncertain in the
> decisions undertake a lot of things and nothing
> them it succeeds. They say that don't be
> successful in their business and, not

---

[51] ERMA, *Pastore, Similitudini* 63,6. Ed. crit. F.X. FUNK-K. BIHLMEYER-M. WHITTAKER, *Die Apostolischen Väter. Griechisch-deutsche Parallelausgabe*, pp. 454-456. Trad. di A. QUACQUARELLI, *I Padri Apostolici*, pp. 303-304.

[52] ERMA, *Pastore, Similitudini* 63,3-5. Ed. crit. F.X. FUNK-K. BIHLMEYER-M. WHITTAKER, *Die Apostolischen Väter. Griechisch-deutsche Parallelausgabe*, p. 454. Trad. di A. QUACQUARELLI, *I Padri Apostolici*, p. 303.

remembering himself in their heart that they operated badly, they blame the Lord. [53]

Under this aspect affliction becomes a miraculous balm for the souls misled by the dissoluteness because, thanks to the tribulations through which the soul suffers the punishments inflicted by the angel of the punishment, the men, Erma underlines, "*they strengthen himself in the faith of the Lord and, for the remaining days of their life, they serve him with pure heart.*".[54] Beginning from such optics the tribulations, according to Erma, they assume the connotation to be causes that founds a good re-education thanks to which the man is put again in the original condition, brim to live according to the values of the Spirit that are eternal and incorruptible.

The young people can reach such destination, explains Policarpo, if they flees the passions of the world, in how much the meat makes war to the spirit:

> It is beautiful to be detached from the passions of the world, because every passion makes war against the spirit, and neither the fornicators, neither the effeminate men, neither the sodomites will inherit the kingdom of God, neither those people who make strangeness. For this it needs that is distant from all these evil and subjects to the presbyteries and to the deacons as to God and to Christ."[55]

---

[53] ERMA, *Pastore, Similitudini* 63,4-5. Ed. crit. F.X. FUNK-K. BIHLMEYER-M. WHITTAKER, *Die Apostolischen Väter. Griechisch-deutsche Parallelausgabe*, p. 454. Trad. di A. QUACQUARELLI, *I Padri Apostolici*, p. 303.

[54] ERMA, *Pastore, Similitudini* 63,6. Ed. crit. F.X. FUNK-K. BIHLMEYER-M. WHITTAKER, *Die Apostolischen Väter. Griechisch-deutsche Parallelausgabe*, pp. 454-456. Trad. di A. QUACQUARELLI, *I Padri Apostolici*, p. 303.

[55] *Ibidem*

It plays again the thought of the apostle Paul of the fight of the meat against the spirit and vice versa (Gal 5,17). In fact according to the apostle Paul those people who follow the pleasures of the world are not attractive to God because they don't behave as instead he would want and, consequently, they don't inherit the kingdom of God, (1Cor 6,9-10). It realizes itself that the young people are called to do really the educational model of Christ, based on the apathy, that is on the escape from all the passions that the world gets if they leave themselves infatuate. Those people that opt instead to follow Christ are rendered children by him same because they are made themselves to educate from him, in how much they have welcomed his call: "*As a father he called us children and it saved us while we were for losing us*".[56] The calls of Jesus it provokes affliction and pain for the evil clerk previously, for which a new re-education takes foot after a deep contrition sprung by the awareness to have acted badly, whose concrete sign is the tribulations:

> When they are afflicted from every tribulation then to me they are delivered for a good re-education. They strengthen themselves in the faith of the Lord and, for the remaining days of their life, they serve him with pure heart. When they repent themselves then jump in their heart the perverse operas that performed, and they glorify God because it is correct judge and justly each has everything suffered according to his own actions.[57]

---

[56] Ps. CLEMENTE, *Omelia* 1,4. Ed. crit. F.X. FUNK-K. BIHLMEYER-M. WHITTAKER, *Die Apostolischen Väter. Griechisch-deutsche Parallelausgabe*, p. 154. Trad. di A. QUACQUARELLI, *I Padri Apostolici*, p. 221.

[57] ERMA, *Pastore, Similitudini* 63,6. Ed. crit. F.X. FUNK-K. BIHLMEYER-M.

2.2. *The educational model of the true Christian wise man*
2.2.1. Faithful and wise men

The fidelity and the wisdom are two virtues (suits) of the soul that, according to Clemente Romano, are at the base of a life lived to the insignia of a good education that concretely appears since their youth with correct ways: *"We have sent you faithful and wise men, lived in the middle of us with ways corrected by the youth to the old age."*.[58] The dispatch from part of Clemente Romano men's well educated has been depended from the possession, from part of them, of these two virtues, of the fidelity and of the wisdom; virtue that has produced in them correct attitudes, having been living copies of the fidelity and of the wisdom of the Logos that, in primordial Saturday, it was faithful to the Father and to him he turned himself because eternal wisdom of the Father. Under this aspect the fidelity and the wisdom are marked from Clemente as exemplary virtue because those people that have educated to the insignia of these, are living witnesses of the incarnate Truth: *"that they will be witnesses between you and we"*.[59]

2.2.2. Germanic, model of youth

According to the author of the martyrdom of Policarpo Germanico is countersigned as a model of youth because educated to the values of the Christian paideia; paideia that

---

WHITTAKER, *Die Apostolischen Väter. Griechisch-deutsche Parallelausgabe*, pp. 454-456. Trad. di A. QUACQUARELLI, *I Padri Apostolici*, pp. 303-304.

[58] CLEMENTE ROMANO, *Epistola ai Corinti* 63,3. Ed. crit. F.X. FUNK-K. BIHLMEYER-M. WHITTAKER, *Die Apostolischen Väter. Griechisch-deutsche Parallelausgabe*, p. 148. Trad. di A. QUACQUARELLI, *I Padri Apostolici*, p. 92.

[59] *Ibidem*

manifests in Germanic his own power of support toward the weak and of victory against the strengths of the evil through these three virtues: the generosity, the constancy and the highness of mind. The first two are at the base of his support for the Christians that, for their weakness, they bore atrocious torments to already enjoy on the earth the eternal life:

> Taken by the grace of Christ, they despised the torments of the world, purchasing himself, for an alone moment, the eternal life (...). Likewise those that were convicts to the fairs bore horrible torments, spread out on shells and torn with other forms of various tortures, because it try itself of, if it had been possible, to induce them to the abnegation. 3,1 (...). The generous Germanic with his constancy sustained their weakness and it was admirable in the struggle against the fairs.[60]

The generosity, united to the constancy, it is not only to the base of the support of the spirit of that Christians that suffered atrocious torments to motive of their faith and following the incarnate (Christ) truth, but also of their victory against the fairs, brims entirely to satisfy the needs of the meat. For the author of the martyrdom of Policarpo Germanico is marked as the juvenile model of the education, that is of he who he hocks himself, both with the word and with the actions, because the other become strong in the spirit, winning in the struggle against the tendencies of the meat, included the fairs. With his generosity and his constancy Germanic educates the Christians, tormented by

---

[60] POLICARPO, *martirio* 2,3-4.3,1. Ed. crit. F.X. FUNK-K. BIHLMEYER-M. WHITTAKER, *Die Apostolischen Väter.Griechisch-deutsche Parallelausgabe*, pp. 262-264. Trad. di A. QUACQUARELLI, *I Padri Apostolici*, p. 162.

the tortures of the tortures, to sustain the weakness of their body because the suffering of their body induces the spirit to become stronger for being charioteer of the body, or better its coachman.

It recurs the thought of the anonymous author according to which the soul reinvigorates herself and sustains the body when she succeeds to take the reins of its government,[61] or when the body is in prey to the suffering. Germanic it is also a formidable example of victorious educator against the tendencies of the meat, from the moment that the meat fights the spirit and makes him war, taking back the words of the anonymous author of the to *Diogneto*, because this wants to turn it toward the things of the earth: "*The soul loves the meat that hates her, and the limbs: the Christians so also love those people who hate them*".[62] To the eyes of the crowd Germanic it becomes example of highness of mind from the moment that he provoked the fairs to eat him alive:

> The proconsole while it was exhorting him saying to have pity of his youth, him inciting him attracted against itself the beast desirous to get away as soon as possible from this unfair and iniquitous life. 2. Therefore all the crowd marveled of the highness of mind of the pious and generous race of the Christians.[63]

---

[61] *A Diogneto* 5,5. Ed. crit. F.X. FUNK-K. BIHLMEYER-M. WHITTAKER, *Die Apostolischen Väter. Griechisch-deutsche Parallelausgabe*, p. 312. Trad. di E. NORELLI, *A Diogneto*, p. 89.

[62] *A Diogneto* 6,6. Ed. crit. F.X. FUNK-K. BIHLMEYER-M. WHITTAKER, *Die Apostolischen Väter. Griechisch-deutsche Parallelausgabe*, pp. 312-314. Trad. di E. NORELLI, *A Diogneto*, p. 96.

[63] POLICARPO, *martirio* 3,1-2. Ed. crit. F.X. FUNK-K. BIHLMEYER-M. WHITTAKER, *Die Apostolischen Väter. Griechisch-deutsche Parallelausgabe*, p. 264. Trad. di A. QUACQUARELLI, *I Padri Apostolici*, pp. 162-163.

Under this aspect Germanic becomes model of true educator of the Spirit, because, by one side, sustaining the weakness of the meat of the Christians, he shares their suffering that is salutary for the spirit in how much this doesn't stay grasped by the unbridled orgies of this, and because, from the other, he wins on the unfair and iniquitous desires of the meat, freeing the spirit from the jail of this, in to give himself and in to give the body of the Christians to the fairs to be eaten.

Essential bibliography

BALZ H. SCHNEIDER G., *Dizionario esegetico del nuovo Testamento*, vol. 2, Brescia 2004.

FUNK F.X. - BIHLMEYER WHITTAKER M., *Die Apostolischen Väter. Griechisch-deutsche Parallelausgabe*, Tubingen 1992.

QUACQUARELLI A., *I Padri apostolici*, Rome 2000.

Finito di stampare nel mese di Maggio 2015
per conto di Youcanprint *Self-Publishing*